D1051361

THAT REMINDS ME

To *J. B. C. J.*

From *Sandy & Jane*

THAT REMINDS ME

Family Story-Starters
for Passing on the Faith

JEAN BROWN EITTREIM

Augsburg
MINNEAPOLIS

THAT REMINDS ME
Family Story-Starters for Passing on the Faith

Cover and text design: Elizabeth Boyce

Library of Congress Cataloging-in-Publication Data
Eittreim, Jean Brown, 1933–
    That reminds me : family story-starters for passing on the faith /
by Jean Brown Eittreim.
        p.   cm.
    Includes bibliographical references.
    ISBN 0-8066-3623-8 (alk. paper)
    1. Children—Religious life.   2. Storytelling—Religious aspects—Christianity.
I. Title.
BV4571.2.E47   1998   98-9553
249—dc21   CIP

The paper used in this publication meets the minimum requirements of American National Standard for Information Sciences—Permanence of Paper for Printed Library Materials, ANSI Z329.48-1984.   ∞

Manufactured in the U.S.A.   AF 9-3623

04   03   02   01   00   99   98   1   2   3   4   5   6   7   8

To my children
Steve, Julie, David, and Dan Eittreim
with the prayer that you may pass on the faith
to your children.

"Love the Lord your God with all your heart and with all
your soul and with all your strength. . . . Impress [this] on
your children. Talk about [this] when you sit at home and
when you walk along the road, when you lie down and when
you get up" (Paraphrased from Deuteronomy 6:4-7).

And to my grandchildren
Curisa Davison, Aaron, Brandon,
Matthew, Amanda, and Amber Eittreim.
May the faith which first lived in your grandparents,
Orrin and me, and in your father and mother,
live also in you.

My thanks to Agnes Kaasa, a long-time friend, whose belief
in the book and in me sustained me in writing this book. My
thanks also to Debbie Feingold, my friend from Connecticut,
whom I met at a writer's Elderhostel, and whose suggestions
have enriched and clarified this writing in wonderful ways.

Contents

THAT REMINDS ME

Introduction

A Story for Brandon

"Grandma, will you read me a story when I get ready for bed?" ten-year-old Brandon asked.

"Get your 'jammies' on, and I'll be right up," I answered. I wondered if this was the night to try out one of my story-starters.

"How about if I *tell* you a story tonight, instead of reading one?" I asked as we arranged ourselves comfortably against the pillows.

"What's the story about?"

"You can choose," I offered, running my finger down the table of contents to find the two I had marked. "Do you want to hear about the day you were baptized or a trip we took when your mom was a little girl?"

"The day I was baptized," he quickly responded.

"Okay," I said, pausing to recall images from that day ten years ago. "Your mom wanted you to wear the dress she had worn when she was baptized."

"Dress!?" he interrupted.

"Well, yes, boys sometimes wore special dresses when they

were baptized. And this dress was one your mom's grand-mother had worn when she was baptized."

"You mean Grandpa's mother? It must have been really old."

"Yes, it was old and very fancy. It was a long dress. It would come way down to here." I showed him with my hands. "But you were too big for it. Your mom couldn't get the dress buttoned. She bought you a little white suit instead.

"You know Agnes and Bob are your godparents. Your mom chose them because they had always been like angels to her, loving her and reminding her of God.

"And Grandpa Eittreim was the one who baptized you. It was very special for him. I could tell by the way he looked at you. He loved you so much."

"I still miss him," Brandon responded.

"I know you do. And so do I." We were both quiet for a minute before I continued.

"Well, Grandpa lifted some water in his hand and poured it on your head. And then he said, 'Brandon Lloyd, you are a child of God.' I know he was praying you would always remember that—that you *are* a child of God."

I gave him a hug and breathed a contented sigh. I had told my first faith story to Brandon. It had felt good. I liked reminding Brandon about being a child of God. And I could tell Brandon had enjoyed it.

I began thinking about the next faith story I'd tell Brandon—and ones for Curisa and Aaron and Matthew and Amanda and Amber.

Maybe their parents would enjoy hearing the stories, too.

What is a faith story?

It is my story; it is your story—the story of our lives. More than that, it's the story of what we believe. It's the story of where we get our strength and our direction for living. Our faith story is the story of our journey through life with God.

Why tell faith stories?

Thousands of years ago, clans gathered around campfires to hear stories of the past—stories about finding a spouse or the birth of a child, stories of epic battles and great floods. As the children listened, they learned who they were and what kind of people they were expected to be. They learned the values and beliefs of the clan.

In the tents of the biblical patriarchs, in the shadows of Egypt's pyramids, under the skies of Canaan, God's people told stories. Stories about creation and the Creator, tales of a great flood and a promise, stories about ancestors who became

Children of Israel—and children of God. The story of Abraham and Sarah was repeated from generation to generation. God had led Abraham and Sarah to a new land. God had given them a son in their old age. This story reminded the listeners that they were to trust God as Abraham and Sarah had done. It gave them confidence that God would bless them. It reminded them of their responsibility to be a blessing to others.

Even when I was growing up, storytelling was common among families. Nearly all of my grandparents, aunts, uncles, and cousins lived in the same community. We often gathered on quiet Sunday afternoons, and while eating pie and playing ball, we listened to stories. I heard how my grandpa picked corn for a neighboring farmer who had been injured in an accident. When my grandmother's sister-in-law died in childbirth, I heard Grandma say she felt it was God's will that she raise her sister-in-law's children. At age sixty, she adopted all four of them. We children overheard these stories as we played or ate nearby. We began to realize that we belonged to a family who helped others and who trusted God. Those powerful messages have stayed with me all my life. Years later, when my husband and I adopted three children, my grandmother asked, "Are you following in my footsteps?" Subconsciously I probably was!

We tell faith stories because we want to pass on our faith to our children. Like the clans' stories long ago, our stories tell our children what kind of people they come from and what kind of people we expect them to be. And as Abraham and Sarah's story inspired people to trust in God, our own faith stories inspire our children to trust that same God.

Will children listen?

Children love to hear stories—especially when the storyteller is someone who knows and cares about them. And when such a person puts aside time to be with them and share stories with them, a wonderful bond is formed between the listener and the storyteller.

Children are powerfully influenced by all the many stories they hear, whether those stories come from loved ones or from television, movies, and the pages of newspapers and books. From the stories they hear, children learn what kind of person is perceived as a winner or loser. They learn what others value as important in life. They learn where people put their trust when faced with danger. And from stories, children begin to decide what kind of people they will be.

Young people especially love to hear stories about themselves. They love to look at clothes they wore when they were very young and hear about adventures they had while wearing those clothes. They love to hear how proud you were the day they learned to walk, and the day they recited their first memorized verse in Sunday school. Such stories give the child a sense of identity and a sense of confidence. They tell the child she is loved, that she is capable.

Children also want to hear stories about their family. This is how they will learn the goals and values that have guided their family's life. Family faith stories will also teach them about the God who has guided their family through generations. This is how they will learn to value themselves and others as God's creation.

Yes, children will listen to our faith stories. Our stories tell them who they are and who they can be. My ten-year-old grandson asks about his father whom he has never seen: "Was my dad good in baseball?" "Yes, he even had a baseball scholarship," his mother assures him. Smiling, the youngster hurries off to join his Little League teammates, more secure in who he is.

How to Fit a Faith Story into a Busy Day

Several factors make it more difficult to tell faith stories today than in the past. In this age of television, e-mail, CD ROM's, and video games, most of us are not used to telling stories—especially stories about our faith. Our lives are very busy; we need to make time to tell our stories. Adults and children live in separate worlds much of the time; we need to find a way to connect. Grandparents and other family members live far away; we need to find ways to communicate from a distance.

I offer this book as a starting point.

Prepare to tell your story.

Take a few minutes to page through the story-starter suggestions. They are designed for use on all kinds of occasions throughout the year. Within each section are three types of stories, indicated by a symbol below the story's number:

 indicates stories designed for an adult to tell;

 indicates stories designed for a child to tell to an adult; and

 indicates stories for everyone in the group to share.

Each story-starter offers ideas for introducing the stories you tell, for eliciting a story from a child, or for involving a group in swapping stories. Under the topics Bedtime, Mealtime, Birthdays, etc. are suggestions for good times to tell your stories: "Stories to tell while having a bedtime snack," ". . . looking at family photos," ". . . decorating a birthday cake."

Once you are familiar with the content and organization of the story-starters, choose several you would like to try. Mark them so they'll be easy to locate when you are ready to begin.

For the first few times, practice your storytelling techniques. While doing dishes or driving in the car or taking a walk, rehearse the story you have chosen. Imagine your child is with you. Use words that will create pictures in the child's mind. Let your voice convey the feelings of the story. Be careful not to sound preachy.

You may be able to get together with others in your church to practice storytelling. Parenting groups, senior groups, and adult education classes can provide wonderful settings to discuss and practice telling faith stories.

Find a good time.

An important part of preparation is finding the right time to tell your story. That means a time when the child won't be distracted by television or a neighborhood ball game outside the window. You want a time when both you and your listener can relax and enjoy being together. Here are some times that might work for you.

When your child comes home from school. Use this time to re-connect after a day apart. Start with a friendly touch and a recognition of his mood: "You are really excited today!" or "Are you feeling tired?" Encourage him to talk about his day. Then share a little about your day. Follow this with a faith story related to your experiences.

When just the two of you stop at a fast-food restaurant. Eating out with just one child is a special time for me. First of all I am treating the child to her choice of food. And once we are settled in a booth, even though there may be people all around us, it's as if we are in our own capsule. We can focus completely on each other. It's a good time for a faith story.

Mealtime at home. This can be a great time for group stories—especially if everyone is gathered around the table. Here's a chance to involve the whole group in learning about and contributing to family history through the stories they tell and hear. The individual reactions and contributions of each family member will enrich the stories that are shared.

Traveling in a car together. Car trips can be wonderful opportunities for uninterrupted communication. I especially treasure times when I have just one child with me in the car.

Recently I took a three-hour car trip with my ten-year-old grandson. I brought along this story-starter book in its unfinished form. "Choose a story you want me to tell," I said. He paged through the book and finally made his choice: a story about the day he was born. When I had finished, to my delight, he said, "Can I choose another one?" The miles sped by as we shared one story after another.

Bedtime. Perhaps the prime time for sharing stories of faith is at bedtime. This is when a child especially needs to feel secure in the parent's love and the love of God. It is a time to find a quiet corner together. You might hold the child on your lap in a rocking chair or sit close together on the bed. As you tell your faith story, the comfort of your presence and the warmth of your words will assure your child that he or she is safe not only in your love, but in God's love.

In answer to a question. Your child's question may lead to a story: "Where did you get this old spoon, Mom?" You may answer, "It belonged to my mother." Don't stop there. Go on to tell how Mom used it to make a special cake for your tenth birthday. Add a statement of faith whenever you can. "I think Mom considered all birthdays special because it meant God had given us another year to live."

While looking at mementos or objects in nature. Sometimes a souvenir or memento will trigger a story. Bring out your wedding dress, and tell about the day you were married. Take a walk in the garden to look at tulips and talk about how God provides sun and rain and the miracle of growth. My grandson, Matthew, loves maps. Recently I took out a map to show him all the places Grandpa and I had lived. We talked about how God helped us decide where we should live and how God took care of us in each place.

This book can prompt lots of faith stories. You may use the ideas in this book to suggest occasions for many faith stories. Use the table of contents as a guide. Let a child look through the book and select which story he wants you to tell. In a group, read one story-starter from the book and invite each person to tell something related to that story.

Some other times that may be good for storytelling are
- as you do dishes together
- when your child is sick in bed
- when you are preparing for a holiday or a celebration
- when grandparents, godparents or other favorite people come to visit
- when your family takes a hike together

- when you family gathers around a campfire
- and, of course, many impromptu faith stories will be prompted by moods and experiences that arise each day.

Once you have experimented with different times for storytelling, you might consider making one of those times a family ritual. Perhaps Mom or Dad always tells a faith story at bedtime. Or it becomes a tradition to tell group stories whenever the family gathers around the table at Grandma's house. Rituals can be powerful bonding influences in a family. Once you've established a storytelling pattern in your family, the kids won't let you forget it!

Tell stories even when you're far away.

Are you a grandparent who is saying, "I'd love to tell faith stories to my grandchild, but she lives so far away"? Don't let distance stop you. There are effective ways to pass on your stories even when you're miles apart.

Take advantage of visits to tell stories in person. Whenever you have the opportunity, tell faith stories in person. When you're physically present, you can watch the child's reaction. You can put a comforting arm around his or her shoulders. Your listener will retain a much stronger image of the story.

So take advantage of holiday trips and get-togethers to tell stories one-on-one or in groups. Plan stories for July 4th gatherings at the lake or for Christmas dinner at Grandma's. Recently my children and grandchildren were gathered around the table at our lake cabin. I asked each one to tell what they did during the lazy days of summer as a child. I think the children enjoyed the stories as much as we adults did.

Telephone faith stories across the miles. When your child calls from camp needing courage to sleep in a strange place, it may be the perfect time for your own story of fear and faith. If your grandchild lives far away, you may want to make a tradition of telling one story each time you talk on the phone.

Fill your letters with stories. If you like to choose your words carefully, you may enjoy writing rather than telling your stories. Maybe you'd like to illustrate a story or include photos with one. I still remember childhood letters. They arrived on each anniversary of my baptism from my godparent, Uncle Milo, and they were filled with stories. When I was twenty-two years old, I was sick with cancer and given only eighteen months to live. It was then that I received a very special letter from my grandmother. Along with a story of faith, she wrote: "I believe you will not die. God has more work for you to do on this earth." This message was certainly a part of my miraculous healing forty years ago, and it remains with me today.

E-mail faith stories. Some of you will write your stories on a computer and send them via e-mail. When your godchild in a distant city is on your mind, send him a quick and brief story via e-mail. Or if your child is away at college, include a faith story when you communicate by e-mail.

Record and send your stories via audio- or videotape. While you are telling a story to your grandchild who lives nearby, you can record it on cassette for the grandchild who lives far away. Or you may chant or sing a simple story onto a tape for very young listeners. When I was a first-grade teacher, I discovered that the children never listened better than when I chanted my message. I just made up a sing-songy tune as I went along. The room became quiet and relaxed. Everyone listened. Consider making this kind of tape for a toddler to use at bedtime.

Or record a story on videotape. At Christmas or other special occasions, use your camcorder to capture several people telling faith stories. Preserve these stories for the family to enjoy years later.

HOLIDAYS,
HOLY DAYS,
SPECIAL DAYS

New Year's Day

Stories to tell while
- gathering for a family night on New Year's Eve
- watching family videos from the year just past
- looking through the family photo album
- gathering for a meal on New Year's Day

 Invite everyone to tell about one unexpected blessing that came to them in the past year. Light a candle on a New Year's cake for each blessing. Blow up and hang a balloon for each blessing received. Invite each person to draw a picture or symbol of the blessing. Display the pictures or make them into a book of blessings.

2 Play a game to celebrate blessings (best for a group of 4 to 24 people who know each other well). Attach a paper plate to each person's back. Everyone writes blessing reminders on the paper plates of others. The

reminders name a blessing that person received in the past year ("You learned to play tuba," "You found a new friend," "Your little sister was old enough to carry out the trash"). When the writing is completed, each person looks at his own plate, chooses the "best blessing," and shares a story about it.

3 Tell about a tough New Year's resolution you made when you were young, newly married, or a new parent. What was the resolution? Why did you make it? How did you try to keep it? Did you pray for God's help? How successful were you? What would you do if you could do it all over?

Valentine's Day

Stories to tell while
- cutting out hearts or making valentines together
- talking by phone on Valentine's Day
- giving or receiving a valentine

 4 Tell about Valentine's Day when you were in fourth or fifth grade. Did everyone in class give and receive valentines? Did you help make valentine boxes? Were any kids left out of the hand-outs? Was there someone whose valentine was special to you? Let God enter the story anytime the door opens even a crack—after all, valentines are about love; and God is love.

5 Tell about Valentine's cards or gifts you received from a spouse or friend. If possible show the card or gift. Did you have any valentine traditions? Did your spouse or friend ever forget? How did you feel when this happened? Did you ever forget? This may be a time to talk about forgiving when others don't live up to our expectations, or God's blessing in giving us loving friends.

Lent and Easter

Stories to tell while
- dyeing Easter eggs
- preparing special foods together
- setting the Easter dinner table with a child or grandchild
- eating dessert at the Easter meal

6 How did your family prepare for Easter when you were a child? Did you go to Lenten services on Wednesday nights? Did you "give up" anything during Lent? What was the general mood of this season? What spiritual value do you see in those Easter preparations?

7 How did your family observe Good Friday when you were growing up? What did you do? What was the weather was like on those Fridays? (Growing up in Decorah, Iowa, I remember Good Fridays always being cold and rainy. Somehow this seemed appropriate for the occasion.) How did you feel about your Good Friday observance? What did it mean to you?

 What made your childhood Easters special? Tell the story of a typical Easter Sunday. Did you wear special clothes? Did you have colored eggs or baskets? What was the weather like? Did you get up for sunrise services? What spiritual meaning did you attach to Easter as a child? How has that changed or remained the same over the years?

What is your favorite Easter hymn or spiritual song? If possible, sing or listen to it together. When did you first learn this song? Tell why it is important to you.

Mother's Day

Stories to tell while
- helping your child make or shop for a Mother's Day gift
- traveling to visit Grandmother on Mother's Day
- talking on the phone on Mother's Day
- receiving a gift or card from your child

10 Tell about Mother's Day traditions when you were growing up. Did you make a gift or card for your mom? Did you buy a gift? Did you offer to do something as a gift? What were the best gifts you gave your mother? Did you see your mom as a gift from God?

11 If you are a mother, tell how Mother's Day has affected you. Recall things your children did that especially touched you. Tell how you have felt about yourself as a mother. (I remember sometimes feeling totally inadequate to the task. It's okay to admit this to your children.)

12 Invite everyone to tell one thing about their mother or grandmother that they would like to emulate. Tell stories that show how she demonstrated this characteristic.

Memorial Day

Stories to tell while
- watching a Memorial Day parade
- decorating a grave site or visiting a cemetery
- writing a letter to someone dear who has died

Because Memorial Day originated to honor people who fought in wars, tell stories about a war you remember. Show pictures or memorabilia or listen to a song from the time of the war. How old were you at the time? Did you know anyone who fought in the war? What was the attitude toward the war in your community? In your church? How did you feel about the war?

Tell a story as you decorate grave sites together. Without words, this act demonstrates love and appreciation for the person who has died and for the past. It tells children that in this family, people are not forgotten when they die. Tell stories about the person whose grave you decorate. Tell about their beliefs, their faith, their deeds.

15 Create a story together as you write to someone who has died. Memorial Day may trigger renewed feelings of sadness and loneliness for children who have lost parents or someone dear. You may decide to write a letter together to one who is gone. Start with sentences like "I remember when . . ." or "I wish we could . . ." Then add "I will always love you because . . . " Close with a statement of faith such as "I'm glad God gave me you for a dad," or "I know you are in God's care."

Father's Day

Stories to tell while
- making or shopping for Dad's gift
- going fishing or golfing together
- traveling to see Grandpa
- writing a card for Dad or Grandpa
- gathering to celebrate Father's Day

 16 Tell about Father's Day when you were growing up. Did you make or buy a gift and card for Dad? Did you offer to do something special as a gift? What was the best gift you ever gave your father? Did you see your dad as a gift from God?

17 Tell a story about your life as a dad. Talk about something your children did that especially pleased you. Or tell about when you felt most proud of being a dad. Tell about prayers in which you got help being a father.

18 Invite everyone to tell one thing about their father or grandfather that they would like to emulate. Tell a story that illustrates that characteristic.

19 Invite everyone to tell a humorous story about something that happened to their father or grandfather. Recall something he forgot to do, something ridiculous or silly he said, a time when his words were inconsistent with his actions. Children need to hear mistakes parents have made and funny things they've done.

20 Tell an open-ended story about Dad, with the child filling in blanks. "Close your eyes and imagine a story about your dad. Imagine he is coming home from work. Where are you waiting for him? What does his face look like? The first thing he says to you is . . . Think about something you want to show your dad. What is it? What does he say about it? How does that make you feel? Think about something you have always wanted to say to your dad. Say it now. How does it make him feel? What does he say to you?"

Independence Day

Stories to tell while
- waiting for the fireworks to begin
- roasting marshmallows for "S'mores"
- sitting at a picnic table, on a porch swing, on the steps of your house

21 Tell about fireworks at other times and in other places. What was the most unusual place you watched fireworks? What was the most romantic occasion? What was your worst experience? (I remember great hordes of mosquitoes!)

22 Tell about your favorite patriotic song. Sing your song together or listen to a recording. Consider "The Star-Spangled Banner," "My Country 'Tis of Thee," "God Bless America," "America the Beautiful," and others.

When did you first hear or sing this song? What attitudes and beliefs does it reflect? Which words are important for you today?

Summer Vacation

Stories to tell while
- sitting on the porch swing or under a tree
- visiting the home where you grew up
- helping children plan a summer day
- traveling to a summer outing or to visit relatives or friends
- telephoning or writing a child who's away for the summer

23 Tell what you did on lazy summer days when you were a kid. Tell lots of stories. Did you build tents or forts? Did you put on plays or circuses? Did you sell lemonade or shine shoes (as my kids did)? Did you play with neighbor kids or by yourself? Did you explore a park? A creek? Did you have a tree to climb? What was your favorite summertime activity?

24 Tell about trips into nature you took with your family. Did you go to the beach, the mountains, the lake? How long did you stay? What did you do in the car on the way? What did you pack to take along? What did you do when you got there? What impressed you most about God's creation?

25 Tell about childhood visits to relatives or friends. Which were your favorite visits? How did you spend the time? What was different about their family life from your own? Did you get special instructions about behavior? Looking back, what could you observe about their belief in God?

26 Tell about places you stayed without your parents. What was your scariest night away from home? How did you get in trouble when you were away from home? What skill did you learn that your parents would never have taught you? Remind the child—and yourself—that wherever you go, God is with you.

Back-to-School Days

Stories to tell while
- getting ready to send the kids off to a new school or new school year
- planning clothes or supplies for a new school year
- visiting together the school you attended as a child

27 Tell about your first day of school (in kindergarten or any other year). What clothes did you wear? Who went with you? How did you feel about going to school? What did you like best that first day of school? (I loved the smell of new crayons!) Looking back, how do you think God went with you that first day—and first year at school?

28 Tell about your worst day in school. Was there a terrible test? A mean kid? A teacher who didn't like you? Did you talk to anyone about it? (God?) How did you cope? Often sharing our vulnerability will encourage the child to do the same. Then we can remind the child (and ourselves) that even when we can't tell anyone else a problem, we can tell God. And God can help.

Halloween

Stories to tell while
- planning or making a Halloween costume
- admiring a child's costume in person or as shown in a photo or video

29 Let the child tell a story in answer to "What do you want to be?" It's Halloween. So we expect the child to answer "a tiger," "a cowboy," "an alien." This may be a good time to look for a deeper meaning. "What do you want to be when you grow up?" Encourage the child to build a story around the answer—one describing a home, friends, church, possible spouse, and family; one that explores the kind of person the child wants to be.

30 "Who are you (in this costume)?" This is the child's story. Let them tell you everything about the character. "Would he ever do anything mean? Why? Would he be sorry? Do people admire her? Are they afraid of her? Does she ever help people? What is the best part about him? Is anything about him like you?" (Often children will choose a character very different from themselves.)

Thanksgiving

Stories to tell while
- stuffing the turkey
- traveling to a relative's house
- setting the table
- enjoying pumpkin pie

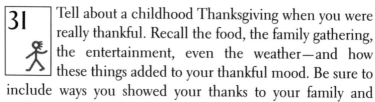

31 Tell about a childhood Thanksgiving when you were really thankful. Recall the food, the family gathering, the entertainment, even the weather—and how these things added to your thankful mood. Be sure to include ways you showed your thanks to your family and to God.

32 For what things in life are you especially thankful? Make this a round-robin story, with each person in the family adding on to a colorful list of thankful thoughts. (In our family we have candy corn scattered on the Thanksgiving dinner table. Each person picks up one kernel for each thing for which he or she is thankful.)

33 Tell the history of Thanksgiving in our country. Do some research, if necessary. Then tell the story of the first Thanksgiving. Imagine you and your family were there, and invite everyone to add details as the story "unfolds" before your eyes.

Advent and Christmas

Stories to tell while
- opening an Advent calendar
- decorating for Christmas
- making Christmas cookies
- shopping for presents
- setting up the crèche

 34 What pleased you most about childhood Christmases? Tell stories about your family gathering, special gifts you gave or received, Christmas music, candlelight service at church. Tell what makes Christmas most special to you now.

 35 Have you ever been disappointed or sad at Christmas? Was someone special missing? Did you fail to get a gift you wanted? Were you ever sick at Christmas? Have you sometimes felt too busy to enjoy Christmas?

36 What makes you feel close to God at Christmas? Special music? Decorations? The closeness of family? Giving or receiving gifts? Quiet times of prayer and meditation? Share a story about a Christmas when you especially felt God's presence.

37 Why is the Christmas story important to you? What meaning do you attach to the birth in a stable? What does the angel's message of "peace on earth" mean to you? What significance to you attach to the wise men's gifts? What do you want the child to remember from this story?

38 What is your favorite Christmas hymn or carol? Sing the song or listen to a recording together. When did you first learn it? Which words are most important to you? Tell why the song is special.

39 Were you in a Christmas pageant as a child? How old were you? Where was it? What part did you play? Did anything humorous or exciting happen during the performance? How was this a spiritual experience for you?

40 What Christmas decorations in your childhood home had a spiritual significance for you? Candles? Tree decorations? Christmas cards? The crèche? Tell what you thought or how you felt about these decorations.

41 What Christmas observances were held in schools you attended? Many adults remember when Christian holidays were recognized or even celebrated in public schools. Tell how it was for you. Invite the child to tell how it is today. Talk about the pros and cons of the differences.

Confirmation or the Anniversary of Confirmation

42 Tell about your own confirmation. If possible show photos, clothing, jewelry, a hymn book, Bible or other objects associated with that occasion. What stories can you tell about your confirmation class or instruction with the pastor? Did you have a special confirmation hymn? Did you answer questions or talk about your faith in front of the whole congregation? Do you remember what the pastor, your parent, or any other adult said to you that day? How was confirmation important to you?

43 Tell an imaginary story about the child's future confirmation day. Give as much detail as you can. Where will it take place? Who will be present? What are your hopes and prayers for the child on that special day?

Birthdays

Stories to tell while
- decorating the cake
- eating a birthday meal
- opening gifts
- getting ready for bed

44 Tell about the day the child was born. What had the family done to prepare for the birth? Where was the child born? Who was present at the birth? What prayers were in your heart that day? What hopes and dreams? Who suggested the child's name? Why was it chosen? Who held the baby in the first days?

45 Tell stories about other birthdays in the child's life. Start with "The birthday of yours I remember best." Let other family members add memories. Focus on the birthday child. Include the spiritual meaning of experiences whenever you can. Then let the birthday child recall his own birthday memories.

46 Tell about a special childhood birthday of your own. What made the day memorable? What was special about that year in your life? Recall things that reflected or expressed your belief in God at that time.

47 Invite the birthday child to record, on cassette or on paper, a birthday story to be stored with photos or mementos in a time capsule and opened next year. Have the child answer the following questions: "What is your full name? How old are you today? What is the most important thing that happened to you this past year? What was the most difficult thing you had to deal with this past year? Tell about someone who helped you this past year. How has God blessed you this past year? What is your biggest wish for the coming year?"

Baptism, Christening, or Dedication Anniversaries

48 Tell the story of the child's baptism, christening or dedication. Show photographs, baptismal clothes, candle, cards, and other reminders of the child's baptism or christening. Where did the ceremony take place? Who was there? Who held the baby? Tell what the observance means to you and to the child. Describe the prayers in your heart that day for the child. Tell this story over and over.

49 Tell about the child's godparents. How did you get to know them? What important roles did they play in your own life? Why were they chosen to be godparents? What do you see as their role as godparents? Invite these people to share their faith stories with your child.

50 Tell the story of your child's name. What does the name mean? Why did you choose it? Who helped to choose it? Was it difficult to agree on a name? How was your faith expressed in the choice of a name? How does the name express your hopes for the child?

 51 Tell the story of your own baptism/christening. If possible show photographs, baptismal clothes, or other memorabilia. What have your parents told you about that day? How were customs different from today? What things remain the same? What did your parents believe about baptism? Tell what your baptism means to you now.

Weddings and Anniversaries

Stories to tell while
- preparing to attend a family wedding
- talking about a young person's wedding sometime in the future
- celebrating a wedding anniversary in the family
- showing pictures or other memorabilia from your own wedding

Tell what love means to you. Tell how you felt about love when you were a child, a teenager, in your twenties, middle-aged, etc. Give examples from your own experience of different aspects of love.

Talk about wedding promises a couple makes to each other. Tell what these promises mean to you. If you are married, talk about some things that have helped you keep these promises.

54 Describe the person you married or that you would like to marry. What characteristics are important to you? What about interests, skills, education, appearance? How important is having similar beliefs in God? Invite the child to tell what characteristics are important to him or her.

55 Tell about meeting your spouse. Where and when did you meet? Tell the story of your first date. What immediately appealed (or didn't appeal) to you about him or her? How were your interests and religious beliefs similar? How were they different? How did your religious beliefs influence your relationship and life together?

Death of a Friend or Loved One

Stories to tell while
- sitting close together
- holding each other
- observing an anniversary or any occasion that reminds you of a person who has died

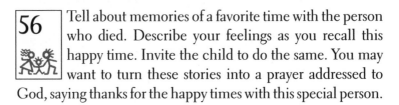

56 Tell about memories of a favorite time with the person who died. Describe your feelings as you recall this happy time. Invite the child to do the same. You may want to turn these stories into a prayer addressed to God, saying thanks for the happy times with this special person.

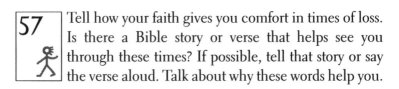

57 Tell how your faith gives you comfort in times of loss. Is there a Bible story or verse that helps see you through these times? If possible, tell that story or say the verse aloud. Talk about why these words help you.

58 Talk about how you see other people expressing their faith in times of loss. What do family and friends say or do that expresses their faith (anything from cards to casseroles)? Look closely and observe the many and varied ways that faith is expressed. Talk about what you see together.

59 Express feelings and questions. Talk about how you feel. Encourage children to talk about how they feel. Talk about questions you all have. It is okay to tell children that there are things we do not know about death. Together with the child or children, turn these expressions and questions into a long, honest prayer to God. Then focus on things that we do know—that God loves us and that we are in God's care.

Death or Loss of a Pet

Stories to tell while
- saying farewell to or burying a pet
- putting away the pet's toys and accessories
- looking at photos of the pet

60 Talk about good memories of the pet. Invite everyone to share a favorite memory of the pet. If this lead to tears, they are healing tears.

61 Invite children to talk about their feelings. Sadness, guilt, loneliness—whatever the feeling, accept it. Share your own feelings, too. There is nothing we can do to take away these negative feelings. But talking about them can reduce their intensity. And including God in the expression of feelings is a reminder that God cares about us and about our pets.

62 Tell about the time your favorite childhood pet died. Describe the pet and what made it special to you. Tell about favorite times with the pet. How did it die? How did you feel? Who comforted you?

SPECIAL
TIMES

Bedtime

Stories to tell while
- turning off the TV and dimming the lights
- sitting with the child on your lap
- sharing a bedtime snack
- making a bedtime storybook for the child

63 Tell about your own bedtime ritual as a young child. How late could you stay up? Did your mother or father tuck you in and read to you? Did someone pray with you? Did you have a favorite prayer that you always prayed? How did you feel about your bedtime ritual?

64 Invite the child to tell about his or her day. "What was the best thing that happened today? Tell two things that made you laugh. Who were your best friends today?" I started asking my granddaughter, Amber, such questions when she was four years old. It felt good to remind her of happy times as she got ready to sleep. It was easy to lead into a thank you prayer.

65 Take turns telling each other about your day. You begin. Tell the best thing that happened, then the worst thing. Then listen to the child's best and worst. Next, tell about a special person who helped make the day good. Tell about two things that made you laugh. This kind of sharing leads easily into praying together about the day.

66 Tell a story the child wants to hear. Using this book, read three story-starter choices to the child and let her choose which story she wants you to tell.

Mealtime

Stories to tell while
- the family is gathered around the dinner table
- eating a leisurely weekend breakfast
- enjoying a favorite dessert
- grabbing a fast-food lunch or dinner

 67 Invite each person to tell something good that happened during the day. Then pray a prayer of thanksgiving. It may be as simple as "Thank you, God, for all the good things that happened today." Or you can sing your thanks. Our family has a thanksgiving theme song:

Oh, the Lord is good to me,
And so I thank the Lord
For giving me the things I need
The sun and the rain and FAMILY!
The Lord is good to me.

68 Invite each person to share a "downer" from the day. A "downer" is anything that makes us feel sad, regretful, worried, or any other negative emotion. Talk about downers only after everyone has told something good. Children's downers may seem insignificant to adults, but our respectful listening tells the children they are important. And children will learn something about adult worlds as Mom or Dad share a downer.

69 Tell about family mealtimes when you were a child. What was your favorite mealtime? Who did the cooking? What was your favorite food? Favorite dessert? For which meal(s) was your family usually all together? Who said the prayer? Was there a certain prayer that you always used? Share this prayer with your child.

Happy Days

Stories to tell while your family is having a happy day—any time at all!

 70 Invite everyone to express their happiness in a metaphor. "I'm as happy as a rainbow." Even young children love to do this once they catch on. The adults can start. You might even want to build your metaphors into happy stories.

71 Invite everyone to name the one thing that makes them happiest today. You may want to celebrate by blowing up a balloon or lighting a candle on a cake for each happy thing. Close by thanking God for joy in your lives.

72 Tell your own personal story of happiness right now. "I'm especially happy today. I went to the doctor yesterday. I had some tests. I was a little worried about my health. But everything turned out OK." Our children will be more prepared to deal with their own vulnerabilities as they participate in ours. And they'll be thrilled that you included them in your happiness. If your child lives far away, share happiness long distance. Perhaps you will begin with "I wished you were with me today when . . . "

Blue Days

Stories to tell while you or anyone in the family is having a down day—whenever the chance arises.

73 Paint a blue story. When children are feeling low, they may be unable or unwilling to talk about it. They may not even know why they feel that way. But they may be able to color or paint a picture of the feelings. You might sit beside them and paint your own picture of feeling down. Just putting dark colors on a page may bring some relief. Do not expect the picture to look like anything you recognize. You may draw out feelings as you inquire about the colors. "Tell me about the purple color." Or "What is the scariest (saddest) part of this picture?" If there is a bright color somewhere, you may use it to encourage something hopeful or happy. If there is no bright color, perhaps you can encourage its addition. "Is there a place for a bit of bright yellow?" Without discounting the child's feelings, you can encourage rays of hope with words like "God wants to bring sunshine back into your life."

74 Tell a story about a blue time you had—recently or long ago. How old were you? Where were you living then? What made you feel "blue"? Did anyone try to help you? What did you do to try to feel better?

Times of Discouragement and Failure

Stories to tell whenever anyone experiences discouragement that comes with failure

75 Give a hug full of positive messages. No words are necessary. The hug will tell wonderful stories. If possible, also take a quiet walk in nature or a private ride in the car with the child who failed. Encourage the child to talk about feelings. Your presence—even in silence—will mean a lot. When the time seems right, offer reassurance—"God loves you even when you make mistakes, and so do I." Or "You feel badly because you struck out. But you're a great kid. You tried your best. And I'm proud of you."

76 Tell your own story of childhood discouragement or failure. How old were you? What did you do? Who was around at the time? How did you feel? Show how your face or body posture looked. What did adults and friends say to you? What helped you feel better? Did God's love and forgiveness help?

Embarrassing Moments

Stories to tell while
- children are blushing—or crying—from embarrassment
- everyone is laughing about someone's silly mistake or foolish behavior

 77 Tell about something that embarrassed you as a child. It may seem insignificant and humorous now, but your child will identify with it. Did someone say something that embarrassed you? Did you do something that made you feel like a fool? Tell the whole story. How did you deal with it? Did you tell anyone about it? Has anything similar ever happened to your child?

 78 Together make a list of embarrassing situations, actions, or words. Ask the child, "What are some things that might embarrass kids?" Add your own list of things that might embarrass adults. This is an easy way to bring up the subject of embarrassment and open the way for stories which may (now) bring chuckles.

79 Invite everyone in the group to tell a "most embarrassing moment." Sharing embarrassing times makes them more tolerable and may help us see them with humor and acceptance. We appreciate knowing we aren't alone.

Scary Times

Stories to tell while
- sitting close together on the bed or on a rocker
- exploring a dark closet or the space under the child's bed
- holding a frightened child—or adult—anytime

80 Give a reassuring hug as you hear the child's story of fear. The fear is almost always real to the child even if it seems unrealistic to you. Listen quietly and patiently to the child's story. You might ask the child what you could do to help. Sometimes more information will help. Explore a dark closet together. If possible, make friends with the neighbor's dog. Read a book from the library about going to the dentist. It is important that we agree with the child that it is a scary situation. We may conclude with a prayer that God will be with us when we are scared.

81 Tell your own story about a childhood fear. Were you afraid of the dark? Of storms? Was there a scary place you did not want to go? Did a surgery or illness scare you? Were there other children who frightened you? Were you ever fearful that a parent would die or that your house would be destroyed? Tell the story of your fear. What did you do about it? What did you wish someone would do? Did anyone help? Ask the child if your story seems like anything that happened to him or her. Listen to the child's story. You may conclude with a prayer that God will help both of you when scary times come.

82 Tell stories about times when it is good to be afraid. Do you remember a time when you were saved from injury by your fear? A time when fear kept you from doing something foolish or wrong? Fear is really a gift from God to help protect us. Together make a verbal list of times when it is good to be afraid.

Sick Days

Stories to tell while
- sitting with a child or adult who is home sick in bed
- visiting someone who is in the hospital

83 Tell about a time when you or someone you loved was ill. Who was sick? Were they in the hospital or at home? What did people do to try to help? Were you worried? Sad? Lonely? How did God help you? How did God help the person who was ill?

84 Tell about childhood times when you were home sick from school. How did you feel about missing school? What was wrong with you? What (if anything) did you miss most about missing school? How did you pass the time?

85 Tell about a Bible verse or Bible story you think of when you or someone you love is seriously ill. You may want to get out your Bible and show where the story or verse is found. When did you first hear this story or verse? Did you read it or did someone tell it to you? Tell the story in your own words or recite the favorite verse. Tell what this story or verse means to you.

Lonely Times

Stories to tell when anyone feels lonely because they miss friends or when they're in a new situation, such as a new school.

 86 Listen to the child's story of loneliness. When children express loneliness—especially because of missing someone—encourage them to say more about it. (You may need to do gentle, patient prodding.) "What would you like to be doing with your friends right now? What do you think they would say to you? Have you changed since you last saw them? What would please them most about you?"

 87 Share your own story of loneliness right now. For example: "I was standing here by the window waiting for you to come. I kept looking and watching and waiting. Then I saw you coming down the street. I was so happy to see you. It's lonely when you're not around." This is not to lay a guilt trip, but simply to share a common, if not so pleasant, feeling.

88 Tell a story about a lonely time when you were a child. Did you move to a new neighborhood, change schools, or lose your best friend as a child? Talk about how it felt. What did you miss most of all in the situation? How did you act and what did you say? Did you tell anyone your feelings? Did you talk to God about them? What happened, finally, to draw you out of your loneliness?

Falling in Love

Stories to tell while
- talking with your child about a special date
- helping your child choose a gift for a special person
- listening to hopes or plans for engagement or marriage

89 Celebrate with your young person who is in love. Listen to her excited story. Affirm her feelings. "You sound really happy." Draw out details of her story and feelings. If possible share your happiness with her. Falling in love brings out the exuberant, child side of us. You may want to ask questions that encourage your child's adult side also. "What do you especially admire about him/her?" "What side of you does he/she tend to bring out?" "Is there any way in which he is like your father/mother?"

90 Tell the story about how your love relationship with your spouse grew. Young people need to hear that most of us did not simply "fall in love and live happily ever after." Tell about how your feelings of love or attraction grew into a relationship. What activities did you enjoy doing together? Which of those activities do you continue to do together? What qualities attracted you? What differences did you discover? How have you dealt with the differences? What has helped make your relationship better?

91 Tell about the qualities you especially appreciate in your spouse. Tell the story of how you came to discover and appreciate these. Why are the qualities important to you? Ask children what qualities they think would be important in a spouse.

Sad Times

Stories to tell while
- any family members are experiencing sadness
- discussing the subject of sadness—as related to a news story, book, movie, the experience of a friend or acquaintance, etc.

92 Tell about the saddest time in your life—either when you were a child or an adult. What made you sad? What was the feeling like? What did you do in your sadness? How long did it last? What made you feel better? Was there a Bible verse or story or prayer that helped you?

93 Encourage your child to tell about a sad time. This story is often easier to tell when the feelings are not acute. It may also be easier if several people are telling their experiences with feeling sadness. "What made you sad? What did you do when you felt sad? What are some ways you showed your sadness? Did anyone try to comfort you? What helped you feel better?"

Times to Say "I'm Sorry"

Stories to tell while
- anyone is feeling guilty
- someone in the family has hurt someone's feelings or caused them to cry
- anyone feels he or she should apologize but is having a hard time doing so

94 Recognize the child's "I'm sorry" story, whether spoken or unspoken. It is never easy to apologize. That's because it is never easy to admit we are wrong. When a young child does something wrong, he knows it, and his face shows it. But he hasn't yet learned how to deal with it. We can help by saying something like, "Did you make a mistake?" Sometimes assurance of forgiveness needs to come before a full confession. (Isn't that what God has done with us?) We may say, "It's OK; I know you didn't mean to . . . " Or "I forgive you; I know you'll try not to do it again." The older child who is more able to verbalize still needs the same assurances of forgiveness.

95 Tell about a time you needed forgiveness. Children need to know that they are not the only ones who make mistakes. They need to hear how we deal with our failures and mistakes as adults. Tell about a time when you sinned—when you hurt someone and needed forgiveness from them and from God. Talk about praying for forgiveness. Then accept the forgiveness and forgive yourself. Your child will be watching to see if you do.

96 Tell your own "I'm sorry" stories to your children. As my children were approaching young adulthood, I recounted to them the shortcomings of my parenting more than once. When one of them said, "We don't want to hear that anymore," I was hurt and disappointed. I didn't realize it then, but there was something I needed from him: his forgiveness. My stories were unfinished; they needed a conclusion: "I am sorry. Will you forgive me?"

When We're Apart

Stories to tell while
- preparing for a separation from a child
- living apart from a child or loved one
- a child is separated from someone she loves

97 Tell the child a story as you give him a keepsake to remind him of you. "Every time you look at this locket, remember I love you. Even though we aren't together, I will be thinking about you and praying for you. I have a picture of you on my refrigerator. Every time I look at it, I'll remember you and pray for you."

98 Write or tape record a story of a happy time you shared with the child. "Remember when we . . . " Tell how the child looked. Tell what you did and how you felt. Perhaps you can conclude the story with a thank-you prayer for the happy times you shared. Send it and, if possible, include a photo of your experience.

99 Tell about being separated from someone you loved. The separation may have been caused by moving to another neighborhood, by a divorce, a death, or some other reason. What did you especially like about the person you were separated from? How did you feel when the separation occurred? What did you miss most about him or her? How did you deal with the separation? What part do you believe God played in the loss or in the recovery?

100 Invite the child who is separated from a parent to recall stories. "What especially happy times do you remember with your dad? What were your favorite things about him? Why do you think he moved out?" (Often children think they are the cause of their parent's separation.) "How did you feel when he moved out?" If possible, assure the child that both parents still love her. Assure her that though human love sometimes fails, God's love is forever.

Times of Success

Stories to tell while
- anyone in the family is basking in the glow of success
- celebrating together the achievements of family or friends

101 Tell a story of some endeavor or task in which you succeeded. What prepared you to succeed? What aptitudes or talents did God give you that helped you? Who instructed or encouraged you? Do you see your success as a blessing from God? Did "luck" play a part in your success? (Do we sometimes call it "luck" when it is really God's blessing?) Talk about the way you felt throughout the experience and in the glow of success.

102 Celebrate children's (or adults') success by encouraging their stories. Listen to the child's story of success. Or share a glowing report you received from a teacher, coach, or friend. Invite the child to tell more about it. "How did you feel when you finished that report or completed that art project? Was it a lot of work? What was the most difficult part? How did you find time to do it? What made you work so hard to succeed? What did you have to miss in order to get it done?" Affirm the child's effort and ability. "You worked hard." "You are really good at _____ ."

Temptations

Stories to tell when
- you sense a child (or adult) is struggling with doing the right thing
- anyone is feeling guilty about giving in to temptation

103 Tell about a time when you were tempted to do the wrong thing. Share stories of your own struggles, temptations, and mistakes with your child. Children and adults need to know they are not the only ones who are tempted or who make mistakes. Tell what you were tempted to do. Why did this action appeal to you? Why did you consider it wrong or inappropriate? How did you decide what to do? How did you feel afterwards?

104 Listen sympathetically to the child's story of temptation. This is a difficult story for the child to tell, and it will be even more difficult if the parent is likely to say, "But you know that's wrong" or "Well, I hope you considered the consequences." Let the child know you understand how difficult the situation was. "It would be hard not to do it when everyone else was doing it." Help the child affirm her own strength: "What helped you decide not to participate?" If the child gave in to temptation and is confessing to it, she probably feels quite a bit of guilt. Avoid heaping on even more guilt with words such as "I'm really disappointed in you" or "You never seem to learn." Instead, strengthen the child for future temptations by asking, "What will you do next time?"

Anger and Frustration

Stories to tell when

- anyone is about to lose his or her temper
- anyone has lost his or her temper
- a family member is obviously angry or frustrated or holding a grudge

 105 Help the child tell his story of anger or frustration. Be gentle. "You look angry. Are you angry? Do you want to tell me about it?" The child's story may not be "reasonable." (Anger is often unreasonable.) Difficult as it may be, it's important to acknowledge and accept the child's anger. However, it's equally important to calmly point out—and stop—inappropriate angry behavior: "It is not okay to bang the kitchen chairs around. Do you feel like riding your bike for awhile or going into your bedroom and beating on a pillow?" Later, when the child has calmed down, you can help him list options for ending his anger stories in more effective ways. These options must focus on what the child can do, not what the other person should do.

106 Tell about a time when you were angry as a child. What made you angry? How did you react? How did other people deal with your feelings? Why has this incident stayed in your memory so long? (I will never forget how angry I was one day when I was five years old. The doctor had come to treat my baby sister who was sick with pneumonia. He was in the bedroom with Margaret, my mother, and my dad. I heard Margaret screaming as I waited outside the door. I thought the doctor must be hurting her, and I became angry and scared. When the doctor came out, I took matters into my own hands and bit him.

107 Invite everyone in the group to tell about a time when they were angry as a child. You will need to sense when your group is ready for this one. Most of us do not like to talk about our anger. Let anyone "pass" who does not want to tell a story. However, if your group is willing to share, you'll probably all get a laugh out of seeing how serious we get about our anger. Maybe you will go on to talk about a bit of wisdom from the Bible: "Be angry, and sin not." (Ephesians 4:26)

When Life's Not Fair

Stories to tell when anything unfair and upsetting happens to someone in the family.

108 Invite the child to tell the story of how he or she was treated unfairly. "What were you doing? Who was there? What did they say? What did they do? How did you feel? What did you do next? How did things turn out?" Perhaps you will compliment the child on handling the situation well. Or help the child think of options for next time. You may want to assure the child that God wants her to be treated fairly and so do you.

109 Invite everyone in the family to tell about a time they were treated unfairly—perhaps falsely accused or unjustly ridiculed. "What happened to you? What did you do? How did things turn out?" Hearing different people's answers helps us know we are not the only ones to suffer injustice. It also makes us aware of more options we might use in such situations.

110 We need to be careful not to interrupt a child's story with our own memories. It may be best to wait until later in the day before saying, "Do you want to hear about the time I was treated unfairly?" (Never try to top their story: "You think that's bad? Listen to what happened to me!") If the child's answer is positive, recall what happened to you. How did you feel? What did you do? Who helped you? What, if anything, did you learn?

111 Tell an imaginary story about the person who acted unfairly. This is the kind of story that may help the child better understand the other person's behavior. If the troublesome person was a child, the story might go something like this. "Maybe [Jimmy] started out the day by deciding to wear his older brother's shirt. His sister made fun of him because he looked funny in that big shirt. Then his mother scolded him for wearing his brother's shirt.

Then his brother hit him because he had taken his shirt. He came to the park where you were playing ball. He wished he could be on a team but the teams were already chosen. He thought you probably wouldn't let him play, so instead of asking he just made fun of you. Do you think something like that might have happened?" Talk about ways the story might have a different ending.

SPECIAL
PEOPLE

Mom and Dad
(Grandmother/Grandfather)

Stories to tell while
- celebrating a parent's (or grandparent's) birthday
- gathering at a family reunion
- celebrating Mother's or Father's Day
- looking at photos in a family album

112 Tell about a time you really got in trouble and your mom or dad had to come down hard on you. What did you do to provoke the discipline? Did you deserve it? Was your parent's discipline effective?

113 Tell about your mom or dad's occupation. Did you sometimes accompany your parent to work? What did you observe about their work? If one parent remained at home, describe a typical day in their life. What skills or knowledge did you acquire as a result of your parents' work?

114 Tell the story of what you know of your parents' childhoods. Tell when and where they were born, what their parents were like, what their home, neighborhood, school, friends, pastimes were like. If you have photographs or other memorabilia, use these in telling your story.

115 Tell how your parents served God by helping others. Did your mom prepare food for people who were having difficult times? Did she do errands or baby-sit? Did your dad do free work for people who were too poor to pay? Did he help with meals or take people grocery shopping?

116 Talk about your parents' religious beliefs. What beliefs were especially important to them? How did their lives reflect their beliefs? (Tell a story to illustrate this.) What values or beliefs did they especially want you to have? How did they try to teach you these values? How are your own beliefs and values different from your parents? How are they similar?

Brothers and Sisters

Stories to tell while
- celebrating a birthday
- gathering for a family reunion
- sitting around a bowl of popcorn on a winter night

 117 Tell about a scary or dangerous time you shared with a brother or sister. What happened? How old were you? What did you do? How did you and your sibling help each other? Did you pray at that time? How do you believe God helps us in scary or dangerous times?

118 Tell about a secret you shared with a brother or sister (if this is acceptable now). What was the reason for the secret? Who told and who kept the secret? How long were you able to keep it? What was the result of keeping the secret?

119 Tell a story about characteristics or skills you especially admire in your brother or sister. When did you first discover those characteristics? What made you admire them? When did you feel proudest of your sibling because of those skills? Which characteristics do you and your sibling have in common? Which characteristics in your sibling do you think God admires most?

Grandparents, Aunts, Uncles, and Cousins

Stories to tell while
- traveling to visit a relative
- opening and reading a letter or Christmas card from a relative
- looking at photos of a relative

120 Tell about a trip your relative has taken. These stories may range from Grandpa going to town by horse and buggy to a cousin traveling to Vietnam. Where did they go? (If possible show it on a map.) How did they travel? How far was it? What was the purpose of the trip? What were some of the trials or blessings of the trip? How would you have felt if you had been along?

121 Tell about a hardship, illness, or difficulty your relative has coped with. What happened? How old was this person at the time? How were conditions different from today? Where were you or what part did you play in the events? What do you admire about the way this person coped with the difficulty? Do you believe God had a part in the outcome?

122 Tell about a favorite time you had with this relative. How old were you? What did you do together? Why was this special to you? How has this relative influenced your life?

123 Tell about a time your relative helped you or taught you something. What were the circumstances surrounding this event? What prompted the relative to help? How did you feel about the help or lesson at the time? How did you respond? Do you see this person's action as one of God's gifts in your life?

Neighbors Near and Far

Stories to tell while
- sitting on the front porch together
- walking through the neighborhood
- discussing important national and international news events
- visiting childhood neighborhoods

124 Tell about a neighbor who was especially important to you as a child—or to your family. If possible show a photo of the neighbor or point out the neighbor's house as you visit your childhood home. What did the neighbor do for you or with you that you appreciated? What did you do for the neighbor? Are relationships with neighbors different nowadays? Is there anyone in the child's life who can be a mentor neighbor?

125 Tell about a friend or "neighbor" you met in another city or country. Show a photo or an object associated with that person. Tell the story of how you met and what you learned from this person. Why is he or she important to your life? How is this person's life different from yours? How are this person's values similar to yours? Remind the child that God loves every person in the world. Perhaps you will talk about how God might want us to show love to other neighbors who live in distant lands.

Favorite Teachers

Stories to tell while
- getting ready for a new school year
- celebrating a good report card
- choosing a gift for a special teacher

126 Ask the child to tell a story about his favorite teacher. "What was the teacher's name? What grade or subject did he or she teach you? Why was this teacher your favorite? What was the most amusing, fun, surprising thing that happened while you were in his or her class? What was the most important thing you learned from this teacher? How do you think this teacher was serving God by the way he or she taught you?"

Tell about your favorite teacher. If possible show a photo, a yearbook, an old school paper, or a report card. Ask the child to guess what made this teacher so special for you as you tell all the details you can. What did this teacher look like? What kind of car did he drive? What made the teacher's classroom look/smell/feel special? What idiosyncrasies did she have? How did the other students feel about him? What was homework like? Tell a favorite/amusing/surprising experience you had with that teacher. When you have finished your story, ask the child to guess what made the teacher special to you.

Good Friends, Best Friends

Stories to tell while
- showing your children pictures from your childhood
- listening to your children tell about good times with friends

128 Tell about a school friend with whom you discussed life's important issues. If possible show a photo of your friend. When and where did you meet this friend? What were some activities you did together? What did you like best about him or her? Tell a story of an exciting or frightening experience that drew you closer together. What important life questions did you discuss? How did your Christian beliefs influence these discussions?

129 Ask the child to tell a story about her best friend. "What do you and your friend like to do together? In what ways is your friend like you? In what ways different? In what way is your friend a good influence on you? What makes this friend your best friend? Tell a story about a really fun or exciting time you had together."

People at Church

Stories to tell while
- having Sunday dinner after church
- sitting together at a church picnic or social

130 Tell about a person at church who influenced you as a child. Talk about what church was like when you were growing up and how that person made church special for you. What was your relationship to this person? If possible, recall and tell about a specific incident involving him or her. How old were you at the time? How did that person affect your life and your attitude toward church and God?

131 Invite the child to tell stories about people he likes to see at church. "Who teaches you the most about God at church? Who makes you feel special at church? Whom do you have fun with at church? Do you do anything to help others at your church?"

Heroes from History, Literature, and the News

Stories to tell while
- talking about a movie or book together
- discussing a news story about a celebrity or popular hero
- checking a child's homework assignment in history

132 Invite the child to talk about a character she admires in a movie she has seen or a book she has read. "What did this character do in the movie or book? What did you especially admire about him or her? Is that the kind of person you would like to be? Tell a story about what you would do if you could be that character. What would be difficult about being that kind of person?"

133 Tell about a favorite book you enjoyed when you were younger. How old were you when you read it? Did you have a favorite time and place for reading? What made the book special to you? Perhaps you will even want to read the book together. You may want to ask the child to guess which character you admire the most. What characteristics does this person possess that are important to you? Do these qualities have anything to do with your beliefs about God?

134 Tell a story about a personal hero that relates to your child's history lesson in school. Your personal stories can make history come alive for your child. If your child is studying World War II, tell him about a relative who was a pilot in that war. If possible show pictures or memorabilia from this relative. Talk about the beliefs and values that guided your relative and his or her family at that time.

135 Relate national holidays and historical incidents to your own personal story. For example, January 15 is the national holiday celebrating the life of Martin Luther King, Jr. Tell your child what you remember about the day King was killed—if you were living then. What were you doing? What injustices was he trying to overcome? What message did he use to try to change conditions in our country?

136 Relate a news story about a national figure to your own personal beliefs. Watch a news story on TV or read a story in the newspaper together. Then expand the story by talking about it. How does God fit into this story? Do you think each person in the story feels that God loves him or her? Which person or persons in the story believed they were doing God's will? Which would you call "heroes"? What do you think would be God's will in the story? Do you believe God would want you to do anything in response to the story? Invite the child to think through these questions with you.

137 Tell the story of a political figure, a sports hero, or a movie star who was your hero as you were growing up. What did this person do that made him or her famous? Why did you admire this person? Invite the child to tell about his or her hero.

138 Invite each person to tell about someone from history that he or she would like to meet. What made this person famous? What impresses you about this person? What spiritual values do you think this person had? What questions would you like to ask this person?

SPECIAL
PLACES

Church and Sunday School

Stories to tell while
- talking about what happened in Sunday school
- taking a walk through your church when it's quiet and empty
- visiting the church you attended as a child

139 Tell about your earliest memory of Sunday school or your first Sunday school class. How old were you? Who brought you to Sunday school? How did you feel about going? What did your room look like and smell like? What do you remember about your teacher? What stories do you remember? What songs?

140 Talk about a church building that was important in your past. If possible, visit the building together or look at a photo. Did your family have a certain place to sit? What pictures, symbols, windows, or other visuals impressed you as a child? What sounds do you remember? What smells? What did you do during the sermon when you were really young?

141 Tell about church activities that were important to you as a teenager. Did you sing in a choir? What social activities did you participate in? Did the church youth group go on trips together? Did they have study groups for young people? What influence did these youth activities have on your life?

School

Stories to tell while
- preparing for a new school year or marking the end of a year just finished
- visiting your old home town and neighborhood
- talking about the "good old days"

142 Tell about your elementary school. If possible show a photo of yourself as a child outside this building. How large was the building? Where was it located? What was it like on really hot and really cold days? How did you get to and from school? What games did you play at recess? How did your room look different from today's classrooms?

143 Inspire your child to dream about college. If possible, take your child for a walk around your old alma mater. Tour the campus and describe your activities in each location. Ask the child to guess where you spent most of your time. If a campus tour is not possible, substitute your yearbook.

On the Road

Stories to tell while
- traveling together by car or train
- viewing souvenirs and snapshots of family trips
- helping a child prepare for a class or church trip

144 Describe a class trip you took in elementary school, high school, or college. Tell about the trips you especially remember. Did you travel as a member of a sports team? Did you take trips to music or drama events? Who went with you? How did you get there? What did you do on these trips? What humorous or exciting things happened? What was best about these trips?

145 Have a "show-and-tell" after a family trip. Show a video, slides, photos, postcards, and souvenirs of a family trip. Let everyone join in to tell the story. Some questions to ask might be: What was your favorite place on that trip? Who was the most interesting or special person you saw on that trip? What was most difficult or boring about the trip? How did that trip influence your life?

146 Let each person tell about a trip that was made special by what happened on the way. Did you ever drive off and leave someone behind? (We left one of our children at a rest stop once! The other kids soon noticed they had too much room in the back seat.) Were you ever in an accident or near miss? Did you ever lose your way?

Lakes, Seashore, and Mountains

Stories to tell while
- enjoying a family holiday
- viewing memorabilia or photos of a family vacation
- planning next year's vacation

 147 Tell about a happy family time at a lake. Describe the setting in detail. What sounds did you hear. What smells? Recall sunny and stormy times by the lake. What made this family time special?

148 Tell about a special time at a seashore. Describe the weather, the sounds, the smell of the air and the sea, the feel of the sand and the water. What did you find as you strolled along the beach or waded into the water? Tell what was special about this time. Is there any way in which the seashore reminds you of God?

149 Tell a mountain story. Your story might be about a real mountain or a "mountain-top" experience. It might be about climbing a mountain or about overcoming a mountainous challenge. What did you discover about mountains that you had never before considered? Did God play a part in your mountain story?

Camp

Stories to tell while
- children are preparing for or recently back from a camping trip
- sitting around a campfire with the family

150	Tell about a Bible camp, a youth gathering, or an outdoor education experience that influenced you. How old were you at the time? Where did the event take place? Who were your best friends during the experi-

ence? What did you discover about the outdoors and your feelings about the outdoors? What messages were important to you there? What decisions did you make at that time?

151	Tell about a family camping trip. Whose idea was it to go camping? How did everyone else feel about the idea at first? Where did you go? What was the most difficult part of the camping experience? What made

the relationships special? What was the best part about eating outdoors? What glories of nature did you experience? In what way was this a spiritual experience?

Visiting Grandparents

Stories to tell while
- celebrating the birthday or anniversary of a grandparent
- looking at old family pictures together
- preparing a recipe handed down through the family
- traveling to visit a grandparent

152 Tell about a happy memory at your grandparents' house. What was your favorite spot there? What were your favorite times to visit? Who was usually there? Recall a wonderful occasion that was part of one of your visits. How old were you? What happened? Why was this special to you?

153 Tell about something you did at your grandparents' house that you couldn't do at home. What was it? Why did you not do it at home? What did you especially like about it?

| 154 | Tell about mealtime at your grandparents' house. What were the best things to eat? What smells do you remember from the kitchen? Did you help prepare any foods? Where were the meals eaten? Were there |

any customs or prayers associated with mealtime?

Secret Places

Stories to tell while
- sitting together in special, secret places

155 Tell about a hiding place you had as a child. Did you hide from your mom or dad when they came home from work? Did you have a place where siblings never found you during games of hide-and-seek? Was there a perfect hideout in your attic or garage? (My best hiding place was to lie on the seats of chairs underneath the dining room table.) Where did you hide?

156 Did you have a secret place to go when you wanted to be alone to read or play or think? Was it a tree house, a meadow, a haymow? Was it somewhere inside your house or garage? (At my grandma's farm, we used to sit in old, discarded cars we found in the orchard.) What did you do there? Who else knew about your special place?

157 Tell about a special place you shared with friends as a teenager. With whom did you share this place? When and why did you go there? Why was it special for you? What important things did you talk about there?

No Place Like Home

Stories to tell while
- visiting your childhood home together
- moving to a new home with your family
- redecorating a room in your home

158 Tell about the home in which you grew up. Describe your favorite activity in each room. Describe how each room looked. What were the familiar smells that came out of the kitchen? What sounds were common in the living room or the family room? What activities took place in the back yard? Where in the house did your family talk about or talk to God?

159 Tell about the home where the child grew up or (if you're a grandparent) the home where the child's parent grew up. Describe the place the child lived when he was younger. What was the neighborhood like?

Who were the neighbors? Describe each room, telling how it differed from his present home. Give lots of details about the child's room. Tell what activities the child did in each room. Point out any furniture, pictures, or decorations from that home that are still in your home. Were there symbols or pictures related to your spiritual life in that home?

 160 Tell the story about moving to a new home when you were a child. How old were you? Why did you move? What did the new home look like? How did you feel about moving there? How did you find a new friend?

161 Invite the child to tell about moving to a new home. "What do you like best about the new home? What was the saddest part about moving? What is scary about moving?" (When I moved to a new house at age six, my bedroom had slanting ceilings because of the roof line. I was afraid the ceiling was going to fall in.) "What did you like best about the old house? What's best about the new home?"

162 Tell an imaginary story before you redecorate a child's room. Ask the child to close her eyes and supply missing words in this story. "My favorite color is . . . My favorite animal is . . . My favorite indoor activity is . . . My favorite outdoor activity is . . . A person I really admire is . . . When I grow up I want to be . . . My favorite thing to remember about God is . . . Something I want in my room to remind me of God is . . . "

Incorporate as many of these ideas as you can in decorating the room.

FAITH

Hymns and Songs

Stories to tell while
- singing songs around the piano
- listening to favorite music together
- decorating for Easter or Christmas

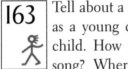 Tell about a favorite hymn or carol you loved to sing as a young child. If possible, sing the song for the child. How old were you when you first sang this song? Where did you first learn the song? Who taught it to you? When did you like to sing it? Why did you like the song?

 Tell about a song or hymn that is important to you today. If possible sing it together or listen to a recording. Which words are especially meaningful to you? When do you like to hear it? Why?

165 Invite the child to teach you a favorite hymn or spiritual song. Be ready for hand motions if your child is young or a drum beat if the child is older. Join in with as much enthusiasm as you can. Try to understand what the words and the music mean to your child.

It's in the Bible!

Stories to tell while
- paging through the family Bible together
- getting ready for bed
- sitting close together for Bible story time or devotions

166 Talk about your favorite Bible verse or story. Find it in the Bible. If you have an illustrated Bible storybook, let the child look at illustrations of the story. Tell why this verse or story is important to you. Then recite the verse and learn it together or read the story aloud.

167 Talk about someone who used to tell or read Bible stories to you. Who read to you? Where did you sit? What time of day was it? What made those story times special to you? Which stories did you like best? Why? If possible show the book that you used.

168 Tell one of your favorite Bible stories. Dramatize the story in whatever way you can. Use different tones of voice, gestures, body posture. Or ask the child to act it out with you. Older children and adults might retell the story in present day language and setting. What makes the story exciting? Who are your favorite characters?

169 Ask your child to retell a Bible story she heard in Sunday school or one you have read to her. Encourage her to use her own words. Young children (under 7) are very literal. To help prompt them, you might use questions like "What happened next?" "What was he doing/wearing?" As children get older, you may begin to probe deeper elements of the story. "Why do you think they did that?" "What was she thinking about then?"

Let's Pray

Stories to tell while
- tucking the child into bed
- traveling together in the car
- gathering around a campfire

170 Tell about how you used to pray when you were a child. Did you have a special time and place to pray? How did you fold your hands? Did you close your eyes or keep them open? Why? Who (besides God) listened to your prayers? Can you think of one certain thing you prayed for over and over? How did God answer that prayer?

171 Invite the child to pray a prayer. He might pray a prayer he has learned by heart or he may make one up. If he needs help getting started, ask a question. "What is the best thing that happened today? What would you like to thank God for right now?"

Invite each person in the group to tell one request they would make of God. What one thing would you ask for yourself today? Would you ask for health, wealth, wisdom, fame, love? Why?

 Invite children to make up a story-prayer. Help them get started by asking questions: "What's the best thing that happened today? Tell God about it. What would you like to tell God thanks for tonight? Who do you want God to bless or take care of tonight? Tell God why."

 Tell stories of thanks for members of your family. When your family is in a reflective mood, perhaps sitting around a campfire or on the shore of a quiet lake, invite each person to tell a story of thanks for someone in the group. "I am thankful to God for [*name*] because you have always encouraged me. One time when that really meant a lot was . . . " If your family is shy about such compliments, give out slips of paper and let them write their stories for you to read later.

Pictures of God

Stories to tell while
- talking about faith around the dinner table
- having family devotions or prayer time
- driving together through the countryside
- having popcorn or cookies

 Talk about how and when you used to think about God as a child? What picture came to mind as you were praying or talking about God? Was God young or old? Gentle or harsh? What was God wearing? Where was God while you were praying or thinking your thoughts? Invite others in the family to share their picture of God when they were children.

 Ask everyone in the group to give three or four words to describe God. A person or a spirit? Inside of us or outside? Judging or loving? Unchanging or growing?

177 Invite everyone to tell one thing in nature that reminds them of God. A towering pine tree? A thunderstorm with rumbles and flashes? Whitecapped green waves pounding on the shore? Tiny pink blossoms? Encourage everyone to describe the natural thing as carefully as possible and tell what they feel about that thing. How does it remind them of God?

178 Talk about how your picture of God changed as you grew older. Tell what you see now as you pray to God or as you read Bible stories or as you talk about faith. How is this picture different from that of your childhood years?

179 Invite everyone to tell about a time when they experienced God's power or nearness or love in their life. Be open to a wide variety of experiences. If some family members come from a different religious tradition, they may describe their experience in words that aren't familiar to you. Listen for the meaning and emotion behind the words.

It's a Miracle!

Stories to tell while
- discussing stories or sermons about biblical miracles
- reading or talking about miraculous events or healings in the news
- praying together for God's help in difficult situations

 180 Invite everyone to tell their favorite miracle story from the Bible. Encourage expression and personal comment during the telling. What makes this story so special to the teller? What is the greatest thing about the miracle? How might something like this happen today?

 181 Invite everyone to tell a miracle story involving God's angels. It might be something that happened in your life or in that of another person. The angel might have come in the form of another person, a dream, or in some other way.

182 What miracle have you experienced in your own life? Think carefully all the way back through you life. You'll probably be able to think of more than one. Choose your favorite. Tell what happened. How did you feel about it at the time? When did you first realize it was a miracle? How has this miracle influenced your life?

183 Invite each person to tell some wonder of the human body that might be considered miraculous. This discussion can help expand awareness of God's loving presence in our world and the presence of God living within each of us.

What We Value

Stories to tell while
- considering family goals and priorities
- discussing news stories about world events
- planning together for the future

 184 Ask everyone—young and old—to name the Christian value they most want to pass on to the next generation. Encourage them to elaborate. How has this value been important to you? Why will it be important in the future? How do you plan to pass it on?

 185 What Christian value was most important to your parents? Tell several stories to illustrate how that value showed in their lives. How did your parents convey its importance to you? How did you respond? Is this value important to you today?

186 Ask everyone what they think is the most important thing to teach children about God and about life. How would you best teach these things to children?

I Wonder

Stories to tell whenever
- your family feels like questioning or dreaming

Let everyone answer the following questions with stories:

 187 If Jesus were preaching in your church next Sunday, what Bible story would he read? What would he say?

 188 If God would want us to change two things about our family, what would they be, and how would God help us change them?

189 What human character from the Bible would you most like to have as a neighbor? As a friend? As a family member? As a leader in our country?

 190 What one thing do you think most disappoints God in the world today? What changes would God like to see?

 191 What is the most important teaching of Jesus for our day? How would the world be different if this teaching were widely followed?

Living Well

Stories to tell while
- putting together a family album
- holding a family reunion
- visiting special relatives
- having a small, intimate "family night" for immediate family

192 Describe a typical day in the life of your grandmother or grandfather. What factors in their lives and surroundings contributed to healthy relationships? What made their lives difficult? How did they work to develop their spiritual lives? What things from their lives would you like to have in your own?

193 Invite each family member to tell about the "best year or decade in your life." What made it such a good time? Who were the important people in your life?

What was family life like then? How was God a part of life back then? What would you like to pull from that time into the present?

 194 Describe your ideal life five years from now. Where will you be living? Who will be living with you? What work will you be doing? What will be your attitude toward life? What will be your relationship to God? What will be the greatest change from your present life?

Led by the Spirit

Stories to tell while
- considering life decisions—large and small
- sharing reflective time together at the close of any family gathering

195 Ask everyone to tell how they prefer to learn about God. Do they like to listen to a sermon, read the Bible, or talk with a friend? What other ways do they learn about God?

196 Tell about a time when you believe God was giving you a message. Was God speaking through a dream, a friend or family member, or an event ? How old were you? Where were you? What happened? What was the message you received? How and when did you decide that God was speaking to you? How has this made you feel about God's direction in your life?

197 Tell the story of how you decided on your career. When did you decide what you wanted to do? What skills or training influenced your choice? How did parents or friends influence you? In what way did God guide your decision?

198 Tell about a significant event in your life that influenced your faith. How old were you? What happened? How did this event influence your beliefs about God and your attitudes toward life?

199 During a family gathering, invite each person to tell one way in which God is active in his or her life today. God's action might be related to health, attitudes, relationships, or goals, etc.

200 Celebrate with your family at the close of any special occasion (holiday, birthday, vacation, or even finishing the Saturday cleaning!). You may want to join hands around the table or give each other a group hug. Invite each person to pray a prayer of thanks for someone in the group. "I am thankful to God for Mom for always loving me." "I am thankful to God for Jeremy's help with the laundry." If your family is shy about group prayers, start by writing the prayers and then reading them out loud. Return to this ritual of celebration over and over, and may God multiply your joy as you pass on the faith.